MY LITTLE BOOK OF DAILY PRAYERS

Bronwen Scott-Branagan

ISBN:
Copyright information:

Acknowledgements:
Thanks to Shan Shan Somerton for suggesting I wrote this little book.

Photographs:
Pages 4, 18, 31: Bronwen Scott-Branagan.
Pages 22, 28: Amanda Thompson.

Table of Contents

PRELUDE 5

MORNING 7

MIDDAY 11

EVENING 13

ANY TIME 15

- PETITIONS 15
- COLLECTS 19
- INTERCESSIONS 23
- MISSION 25
- THANKSGIVING 29

BOOKS BY BRONWEN SCOTT-BRANAGAN .. 32

PRELUDE

Prayer:
Calm me, Lord, as you stilled the storm;
Still me, Lord, keep me from harm:
Let all the tumult within me cease;
Enfold me, Lord, in Your peace. Amen.
(*Celtic Prayer; public domain*)

Meditation:
'God is a Spirit:
and they that worship him
must worship him
in spirit and in truth.'
(John 4: 24, KJV)

Hymn:
God be in my head,
And in my understanding;
God be in mine eyes,
And in my looking;
God be in my mouth,
And in my speaking;
God be in my heart,
And in my thinking;
God be at mine end,
And in my departing.
(*Anonymous, from a Sarum Primer, 1558; public domain*)

Hymn:
Dear Lord and Father of mankind,
Forgive our foolish ways;
Re-clothes us in our rightful mind:

In purer lives Thy service find,
In deeper reverence, praise.

In simple trust like their who heard,
Beside the Syrian sea,
The gracious calling of the Lord,
Let us, like them, without a word
Rise up and follow Thee.

O Sabbath rest by Galilee!
O calm of hills above,
Where Jesus knelt to share with Thee
The silence of eternity,
Interpreted by love!

Drop Thy still dews of quietness,
Till all our strivings cease;
Take from our souls the strain and stress,
And let our ordered lives confess
The beauty of Thy peace.

Breathe through the heats of our desire
Thy coolness and Thy balm;
Let sense be dumb, let flesh retire;
Speak through the earthquake, wind, and fire,
O still small voice of calm!

(*John Greenleaf Wittier; public domain*).

MORNING

Prayer:
I arise today
Through God's strength to pilot me:
God's might to uphold me,
God's wisdom to guide me,
God's eye to look before me,
God's ear to hear me,
God's word to speak for me,
God's hand to guide me,
God's way to lie before me,
God's shield to protect me.
(*From St. Patrick's Breastplate, public domain*).

Hymn:
God has created a new day,
Silver and green and gold.
Live that the sunset may find us,
Worthy His gifts to hold.

God has created a new night,
Silver and dark and still,
Live that the morning may find us,
Ready to do His will.
(*From "Our Chalet Songbook", Our Chalet Committee, Girl Guides Association* 1981)

Prayer:
All through this year, O Father,
Help me to know Christ better
And to make Him better known
By yielding my will

To the Lordship of Christ
And my life
To the service of others,
For Jesus Christ's sake. Amen.

(*Revd. Rupert Charkham, 1990. As the church of St. Mary the Virgin, Sunbury, Vic. prepared for mission and renewal under the guidance of Revd. Andrew Scott-Branagan*)

A Morning Meditation:
My Lord is with me this day,
His glorious presence is around me and within;
His power is in everything I do,
As I take up my tasks, there is a strength
Beyond my own.
As I face life's perplexities there are
Unexpected solutions.
As I face my relationships there is a love
Beyond my own,
Making them sweet and beautiful.
His glorious presence is around me and within.
Alleluia!
(*I have this on a Mothers' Union sheet, but am unable to find the source*)

Hymn:
Take my life and let it be
Consecrated, Lord, to thee.
Take my moments and my days,
Let them flow in ceaseless praise.

Take my hands, and let them move
At the impulse of thy love.
Take my feet, and let them be
Swift and beautiful for thee.

Take my voice, and let me sing
Always, only, for my King.
Take my lips and let them be
Filled with messages from thee.

Take my silver and my gold,
Nothing, Lord, would I withhold.
Take my intellect and use
Every power as thou shalt choose.

Take my will and make it thine;
It shall be no longer mine.
Take my heart, it is thine own;
It shall be thy royal throne.

Take my love: my Lord I pour
At thy feet its treasure store.
Take myself, and I will be
Ever, only, all for thee.
(*Lyricist: Frances Ridley Havergal; public domain*).

Hymn:
Thank you for giving me the morning,
Thank you for every day that's new,
Thank you that all my hurts and troubles
I can take to you.

Thank you for all my friends and helpers,
Thank you for people everywhere,
Thank you for showing me, Lord Jesus,
How to help and care.

Thank you for times of working, playing,
Thank you for all that I can do,
Thank you for all that’s bright and cheerful,
And for music too.

Thank you for comfort in my sadness,
Thank you for all who understand,
Thank you that your hand holds and leads me,
Everywhere I am.

Thank you for speaking to me, Jesus,
Thank you for meeting with me here,
Thank you, because you love all people
Those both far and near.

Thank you that you’re so good and loving,
Thank you that I am filled with you,
Thank you, you make me feel so glad and
Thankful as I do.
(*Martin Gotthard Schneider; translation by D. A. Schubert, public domain*).

MIDDAY

A number of different Christian groups, such as Mothers' Union, suggest that it's a good idea to make a habit of pausing at twelve noon each day to pray the Lord's Prayer. Use the version that you prefer and pray in the language that is your Mother Tongue.

Prayer:
Our Father which art in heaven, Hallowed be thy name.
Thy kingdom come.
Thy will be done in earth, as it is in heaven.
Give us this day our daily bread.
And forgive us our debts, as we forgive our debtors.
And lead us not into temptation but deliver us from evil:
For thine is the kingdom, and the power, and the glory, for ever.
Amen. (*Matthew 6.9 – 13, KJV*)

Meditation:
'Happy are the people who know the festal shout,
who walk, O Lord, in the light of your countenance;
They exult in your name all day long
and extol your righteousness.'
(*Psalm 89: 15 – 16 NRSV*)

Hymn:
Our Father, God in heaven above,
We are your family through your love.
Your name be hallowed: help us, Lord,
To keep in purity your word.
Your kingdom come: yours let it be
In time, and through eternity.

And may your will on earth be done

As it is done before your throne.
Curb flesh and blood and every ill
That sets itself against your will.
Give us this day our daily bread,
Whatever for this life we need.

Forgive us all our sins, we pray:
Take all their burdening guilt away,
As we the sins of those forgive
Who us by their offences grieve.
When testing comes on every hand,
Lord, give us strength that we may stand.

Deliver us from evil days;
Throughout our lives, protect our ways.
And when we die, grant calm release,
And take us home to you in peace.
Thus in your name and at your word
We say: Amen, O hear us, Lord.
(*Martin Luther (translated, public domain*)

EVENING

Prayer:
Dear Prince of Peace,
Please grace me with your peace
In the midst of life
And all its joys and sorrows.
Give to me this evening
Discipline to leave space
For your peace to flow
Into my life.
Strengthen gently and surely
Through your Holy Spirit. Amen.
(*Bishop John Harrower, with his permission, 23/2/2021*)

Hymn:
The day Thou gavest, Lord, is ended,
The darkness falls at Thy behest;
To Thee our morning hymns ascended,
Thy praise shall sanctify our rest.

We thank Thee that Thy church, unsleeping,
While earth rolls onward into light,
Through all the world her watch is keeping,
And rests not now by day or night.

As over each continent and island
The dawn leads on another day,
The voice of prayer is never silent,
Nor dies the strain of praise away.
The sun that bids us rest is waking
Our brethren 'neath the western sky,

And hour by hour fresh lips are making
Thy wondrous doings heard on high.

So be it, Lord; Thy throne shall never
Like earth's proud empires, pass away:
Thy kingdom stands, and grows forever,
Till all Thy creatures own Thy sway.
(*John Ellerton, public domain*)

Hymn:
Abide with me; fast falls the eventide:
The darkness deepens; Lord, with me abide
When other helpers fail, and comforts flee,
Help of the helpless, O abide with me.

Swift to its close ebbs out life's little day;
Earth's joys grow dim, its glories pass away;
Change and decay in all around I see:
O thou who changest not, abide with me!

I need Thy presence every passing hour;
What but thy grace can foil the tempter's power?
Who like thyself my guide and stay can be?
Through cloud and sunshine, O abide with me.
I fear no foe with Thee at hand to bless;
Ills have no weight, and tears no bitterness;
Where is death's sting? Where, grave, thy victory?
I triumph still, if Thou abide with me.

Hold Thou Thy cross before my closing eyes;
Shine through the gloom, and point me to the skies:
Heaven's morning breaks, and earth's vain shadows flee;
In life, in death, O Lord, abide with me!
(*Henry Francis Lyte, public domain*)

ANY TIME

PETITIONS

Prayer:
Arrow Prayers:
Jesus, my Lord and my God!
Jesus, Son of God, have mercy on me!
Lord, just hold me!

Prayer:
O Holy Spirit of God,
Come, live within my heart;
Inspire my thoughts, O Lord,
Draw my imagination apart;
Suggest each single decision;
Order my every doing.
In my silence direct my vision,
and guide my words ensuing,
When working under pressure
and in my times of leisure,
In the freshness of the morning
And the weariness of evening.
Father, relate your grace in Psalms;
In humble worship I rejoice, and then
Abide deep in your loving arms,
Through Christ, my Lord. Amen.
(*B. J. Scott-Branagan, 2021*)

Hymn:
Breathe on me, Breath of God,
Fill me with life anew,
That I may love what Thou dost love,

And do what Thou wouldst do.

Breathe on me, Breath of God,
Until my heart is pure,
Until with Thee I will one will,
To do and to endure.

Breathe on me, Breath of God,
Till I am wholly thine,
Until this earthly part of me
Glows with Thy fire divine.

Breathe on me, Breath of God;
So shall I never die,
But live with Thee the perfect life
Of Thine eternity.
(*Edwin Hatch; public domain*)

Hymn:
Sometimes a light surprises
The Christian while he sings;
It is the Lord who rises
With healing in His wings:
When comforts are declining
He grants the soul again
A season of clear shining,
To cheer it after rain.

In holy contemplation,
We sweetly then pursue
The theme of God's salvation,
And find it ever new.
Set free from present sorrow,
We cheerfully can say,

E'en let the unknown tomorrow
Bring with it what it may:

It can bring with it nothing
But He will bear us through;
Who gives the lilies clothing
Will clothe His people too:
Beneath the spreading heavens
No creature but is fed:
And He who feeds the ravens
Will give His children bread.

Though vine nor fig-tree neither
Their wonted fruit should bear,
Though all the field should wither,
Nor flocks nor herds be there,
Yet, God the same abiding,
His praise shall tune my voice;
For, while in Him confiding,
I cannot but rejoice.
(*William Cowper, public domain*)

COLLECTS

The language of the Collects in the Book of Common Prayer is beautiful. It seems just right for the short prayers that are used in the liturgy, the form of public prayer, placed just before the communion service and also in Morning and Evening Prayer.
For example, a couple of special import are the Collect for the first Sunday in Lent and the one for Easter Day. By the way, there are actually more than forty days in Lent, as Sundays are not counted; they are days of celebration.

Prayer:

O Lord, who for our sake didst fast forty days and forty nights; Give us grace so to use such abstinence, that, our flesh being subdued to the Spirit, we may ever obey thy godly motions in righteousness, and true holiness, to thy honour and glory, who livest and reignest with the Father and the Holy Ghost, one God, world without end. Amen.
(*Collect for the first Sunday in Lent; BCP 1662*)

Prayer:

Almighty God, who through thine only-begotten Son Jesus Christ hast overcome death, and opened unto us the gate of everlasting life; We humbly beseech thee, that, as by thy special grace preventing us thou dost put into our minds good desires, so by thy continual help we may bring the same to good effect; through Jesus Christ our Lord, who liveth and reigneth with thee and the Holy Ghost, ever one God, world without end. Amen.
(*Collect for Easter Day; BCP 1662*)

Hymn (for Lent):
'Forty days and forty nights
Thou wast fasting in the wild,

Forty days and forty nights
Tempted, and yet undefiled:

Let us Thy endurance share
And from earthly greed abstain;
With Thee watching unto prayer,
With Thee strong to suffer pain.

So shall we have peace divine;
Holier gladness ours shall be;
Bound us too shall angels shine,
Such as ministered to Thee.
(*George Hunt Smyttan; Francis Pott. Public Domain*)

Hymn (for Easter):
Jesus Christ is risen today,
Hallelujah!
Our triumphant holy day,
Hallelujah!
Who did once upon the Cross,
Hallelujah!
Suffer to redeem our loss,
Hallelujah!

Hymns of praises let us sing,
Unto Christ our heavenly King.
Who endured the Cross and grave,
Sinners to redeem and save:

But the pain, which he endured
Our salvation hath procured;
Now above the sky He's King,
Where the angels ever sing:

Sing we to our God above,
Praise eternal as His love,
Praise Him, all ye heavenly host,
Father, Son, and Holy Ghost!'
(*Lyra Davidica; based on 14th Century MS; Public Domain*)

Hymn (for Easter):
Thine be the glory, risen, conquering Son,
Endless is the victory Thou o'er death hast won;
Angels in bright raiment rolled the stone away,
Kept the folded grave-clothes, where Thy body lay.
Thine be the glory, risen conquering Son,
Endless is the victory Thou o'er death hast won.

Lo, Jesus meets us, risen from the tomb;
Lovingly He greets us, scatters fear and gloom;
Let the Church with gladness, hymns of triumph sing,
For her Lord now liveth, death hath lost its sting.
Refrain

No more we doubt Thee, glorious Prince of life;
Life is nought without Thee: aid us in our strife;
Make us more than conquerors, through Thy deathless love;
Bring us save through Jordan to Thy home above.
Refrain

(*Edmond Louis Budry,* tr. *Richard Birch Hoyle; Public Domain*)

INTERCESSIONS

These are the prayers we pray when we plead with God on behalf of ourselves or others; it may be the poor, the sick, those suffering from calamity, disease and disaster at home and in countries around the world.

Prayer:
'Beloved, I wish above all things that thou mayest prosper and be in health, even as thy soul prospereth.'

(3 John: 2, KJV)

Prayer:
Dear heavenly Father, we lift up to you all those who are facing illness today. We ask that you would bring healing, comfort and peace to their bodies and minds. Calm their fears and may they experience the healing power of your peace and love. In Jesus' name. Amen.

Hymn:
'What a Friend we have in Jesus,
All our sins and griefs to bear!
What a privilege to carry
Everything to God in prayer!
O what peace we often forfeit,
O what needless pain we bear,
All because we do not carry
Everything to God in Prayer!

Have we trials and temptations?
Is there trouble anywhere?
We should never be discouraged;
Take it to the Lord in prayer.
Can we find a friend so faithful

Who will all our sorrows share?
Jesus knows our every weakness:
Take it to the Lord in prayer.
Are we weak and heavy-laden,
Cumbered with a load of care?
Precious Saviour, still our refuge:
Take it to the Lord in prayer.
Do thy friends despise, forsake thee?
Take it to the Lord in prayer;
In His arms He'll take and shield thee,
Thou wilt find a solace there.
(*Joseph Medlicott Scriven, public domain*)

Hymn:
From Thee all skill and science flow,
All pity, care, and love.
All calm and courage, faith and hope;
O pour them from above;
And part them, Lord, to each and all,
As each and all shall need,
To rise like incense, each to Thee,
In noble thought and deed.

And hasten. Lord, that perfect day
When pain and death shall cease,
And Thy just rule shall fill the earth
With health, and light, and peace;
Whenever blue the sky shall gleam,
And ever green the sod,
And man's rude work deface no more
The paradise of God.
(*Charles Kingsley, public domain)*

MISSION

Prayer:
Lord God, Jesus commanded his disciples: 'Go therefore and make disciples of all nations, baptizing them in the name of the Father and of the Son and of the Holy Spirit and teaching them to obey everything that I have commanded you. And remember I am with you always, to the end of the age.'*

Be with us, Father, and with all who obey that commandment as they teach, heal and share the warmth of your love both in their home countries and around the world. Amen.
*(*Matthew 28.19-20 NRSV*).

Prayer:
Pray the words of Simeon when Mary and Joseph brought the Baby Jesus to the temple:
'Lord, now lettest thou thy servant depart in peace, according to thy word:
For mine eyes have seen thy salvation,
Which thou hast prepared before the face of all people;
A light to lighten the Gentiles, and the glory of thy people Israel.'
(*Luke 2.29 – 32, KJV*)

Hymn:
See how great a flame aspires,
Kindled by a spark of grace!
Jesu's love the nations fires,
Sets the kingdoms on a blaze.
To bring fire on earth He came;
Kindled in some hearts it is:
O that all might catch the flame,
All partake the glorious bliss!

When He first the work begun,
Small and feeble was His day:
Now the word doth swiftly run,
Now it wins its widening way;
More and more it spreads and grows
Ever mighty to prevail;
Sin's strongholds it now o'erthrows,
Shakes the trembling gates of hell.

Sons of God, your Saviour praise!
He the door hath opened wide;
He hath given the word of grace
Jesu's word is glorified;
Jesus, mighty to redeem,
He alone the work hath wrought;
Worthy is the work of Him,
Him who spake a world from nought.

Saw ye not the cloud arise,
Little as a human hand?
Now it spreads along the skies,
Hangs o'er all the thirsty land:
Lo! The promise of a shower
Drops already from above;
But the Lord will shortly pour
All the Spirit of His love!
(*Charles Wesley, public domain*)

Hymn:
Thou whose almighty word
Chaos and darkness heard,
And took their flight,
Hear us, we humbly pray,
And where the gospel day

Sheds not its glorious ray
Let there be light!

Thou didst come to bring
On Thy redeeming wing
Healing and sight,
Health to the sick in mind,
Sight to the inly blind,
O now to all mankind
Let there be light!

Spirit of truth and love,
Life-giving, holy Dove,
Speed forth Thy flight;
Move on the water's face,
Spreading the beams of grace,
And in earth's darkest place
Let there be light!

Blessed and holy Three,
Glorious Trinity,
Grace, love and might,
Boundless as ocean's tide
Rolling in fullest pride,
Through the world far and wide
Let there be light!
(*John Marriott, public domain*)

THANKSGIVING

Prayer:
'You are worthy, our Lord and God,
To receive glory and honor and power,
For you created all things and by your will
They existed and were created.'
(*Revelation 4:11 NRSV*)

Prayer:
'Praise the Lord!
I will give thanks to the Lord
With my whole heart.'
(*Psalm 111:1 NRSV*)

Meditation:
'Be careful for nothing; but in everything by prayer and supplication with thanksgiving let your requests be made known unto God.'
(*Philippians 4.6 KJV*)

Hymn:
Fill Thou my life, O Lord my God,
In every part with praise,
That my whole being may proclaim
Thy being and Thy ways.

Not for the lips of praise alone,
Nor e'en the praising heart,
I ask, but for a life made up
Of praise in every part:

Praise in the common things of life,
Its goings out and in;

Praise in each duty and each deed,
However small and mean.

Fill every part of me with praise;
Let all my being speak
Of Thee and of Thy love, O Lord,
Poor though I be and weak.

So shalt Thou, Lord, from me, e'en me,
Receive the glory due;
And so shall I begin on earth
The song for ever new.
So shall no part of day or night
From sacredness be free;
But all my life, in every step,
Be fellowship with Thee.
(*Horatius Bonar, Public Domain*)

Hymn:
Now thank we all our God,
With hearts, and hands, and voices;
Who wondrous things hath done,
In whom His world rejoices;
Who, from our mothers' arms,
Hath blessed us on our way
With countless gifts of love,
And still is ours today.

O may this bounteous God
Through all our life be near us,
With ever-joyful hearts
And blessed peace to cheer us.
And keep us in His grace.
And guide us when perplexed,

And free us from all ills
In this world and the next.

All praise and thanks to God
The Father now be given,
The son, and Him who reigns
With Them in highest heaven,
The one, eternal God,
Whom earth and heaven adore;

For thus it was, is now,
And shall be evermore.
(*Martin Rinkart, translated by Catherine Winkworth; public domain*)

BOOKS BY BRONWEN SCOTT-BRANAGAN

Adult Colouring Books
Australian Flora and Fauna Colouring Book (Coming).
Words of Wisdom.

Ancestry
Cornish Kinsfolk: From Cornwall to Castlemaine (Prize-winner, 2006; out of print).
Dad, the Great War & Beyond (ibook, Amazon.com).

Bible Study
A Lenten Journey: Paul's letter to the Ephesians (208; 2nd edn. 2014).
Do you Love God? (2016)

Children, 8 – 12years
Joan and the Great Depression (Joan Murray Series 1; 2012).
Joan: Sunshine & Shadows (Joan Murray Series Bk 2 (2015).
Joan: War Declared (Joan Murray Series Book 3; coming).

Devotional
The Practising Christian (2017).
Worship the Lord (2018).

Memoirs
The Memoirs of G. Cutler (2016).
This is Our Story (Our time in PNG 1959 – 1962; 2006).

Miscellaneous
Christmas Card Record Book (2011).

Novel
Balm of Beerburrum (2008; 2nd edition 2016).
Bodrigy (2020).

Poetry
Dithyrambles: Poems of the Heart (2012).

Practical Christianity
The Holy Bible Helpmate (proceeds for PNG Pastors; 2011).
My Little Book of Daily Prayers (2021).
Notes on the Role of the Lay Preacher (2020).

Recipes
An Aussie Dieters' Recipe Book: Simple recipes that are Dairy Free, FODMAP Free, Gluten Free, Lactose Free, Nut Free and Sugar Free – or None of the Above (2018).

Travel
Applegarth: An Australian Family Abroad in 1970 (2014).

Young Children's Books
The Boy Who Couldn't Keep Still (2017).
Chips Quackety (2012).
Christmas Snow (Prize winner, Macmillan Publishing Company, illustrated by author; 2015).
The Pandanus People (Illustrated by author; 2009).

www.ingramcontent.com/pod-product-compliance
Ingram Content Group UK Ltd.
Pitfield, Milton Keynes, MK11 3LW, UK
UKHW060406300726
14090UKWH00006B/462